MY TROLL LIFE

THE TRUE STORY

Original book: Mit Liv som Trold (Danish)

©2022 Jep Andre Laponnel

ISBN (Hardback):   978-87-94335-00-3
ISBN (Paperback): 978-87-94335-01-0
ISBN (Ebook – Kindle): 978-87-94335-04-1
ISBN (Ebook - Epub): 978-87-94335-02-7
ISBN (Audiobook): 978-87-94335-03-4

Published by: Taskforze Danmark ApS

All rights reserved. This book or any portion thereof my not be reproduced without the express written permission of the author.

Website: mytrolllife.com

DEDICATION

I dedicate this book to my mother Lajla for all the support you have given me. To Thomas for making my life so magical and for teaching me seeing the world in a different way.

Thanks to my two daughters Martine and Josefine for always being there for me with patience during my good and bad periods.

A deep loving thank to my wife Hasmik for your fantastic support in every way.

CONTENTS

Foreword	1
How it all began - *The Story of Thomas' Early Years*	5
Lajla Dams story	13
A happy boy with his trolls	21
Life with Grandpa – Thomas Dam	25
My first job at the factory	31
The American	39
The new factory	43
Too many troll copies	49
Thomas leave this world	53
A new troll is born at the troll factory	57
A small troll team	59
The Trolls travels the world	61
The non excisting marketing	65
A Meeting of Cultures	69

We double in size - year after year	73
Really good economy	77
Award for fastest growing company in Denmark, 1993	79
Aalborg European of the Year	83
Danish Marketing Award	85
What comes up…	89
A constant battle on several fronts	95
The complaining never end	101
Taking a break	105
The hunt starts	107
The fire	111
Call from the Police	117
The police trial	123
Forging a new path	129
The movie	131
Conclusion…	135
Am I bitter? No.	139
Thanks to Thomas Dam	141

FOREWORD

Most people have heard of the cute little Troll figures. They are known by both children and adults all around the world. But not many people know the true story behind them. In recent years, a completely different and factually untrue version of the Trolls' story has been created by two people with no connection to the events that unfolded.

In this book I will now set the record straight and tell the true story as it really is from those of us who were there; from those of us who actually created their success.

This book contains the full story about my life as a troll. The story is told through my experiences with Thomas Dam as a father figure. It will tell about how I was raised in the factory, about my years as a director, and how the whole thing just came together from there.

Jep Andre Laponnel

I'll be telling you about the very beginning and about Thomas Dam's youth. Ill also tell you that it actually was my mother Lajla's idea to start mak
ing troll figures.

You will be hearing about the early years' accomplishments and the huge success we had in the 90's, when the Trolls really became world famous.

You also be shown an almost completely unknown side of the Trolls: jealousy, and hatred. And the crazy family dispute that came in the late 90's and that lasted several years. A drama so crazy that you'll hardly believe is true.

Eventually, it all culminates in the film contract with American DreamWorks with the Trolls1 and Trolls2 films.

Although it's a complicated story with the family dispute, and although I don't hold back my critique, I hope that after reading this little book, you are left with the impression of the incredible things that Thomas and Lajla created.

To tell the true story, I need to be completely direct and name everyone involved. I tell the story based on my own experiences, interviews, and my insights into things such as police reports and so on.

MY TROLL LIFE

You might think that my purpose is to shame people but here I will tell you that the things that are in this book are only a small part of what has happened. I'm telling the nice version of the story.

Such is the case with life and with all success stories. There are bright sides and dark sides. Light cannot exist without darkness.

HOW IT ALL BEGAN

The Story of Thomas' Early Years

Already as a boy, Thomas displayed the artistic talent that would later lead to the world-famous trolls. Thomas was born into a very poor fishing family that had no money to buy toys. So little Thomas cut his own toys out of wood. This way, he always had small animals and other characters to play with.

He had trouble concentrating in school and constantly drew characters in his books. This led to beatings from the teacher who wanted him to stop, but nothing worked. The teacher was frustrated and didn't know what to do. He regretted punishing the frail little boy.

One day, the teacher's son saw his grandfather's drawings and said to his father, "Stop beating him. He has talent and you should let him draw". The teacher therefore gave Thomas a small chalkboard and some paper, but he had to promise not to draw in the books. Little Thomas had no problem adhering to those rules.

Just imagine: the Trolls might never have existed if Thomas hadn't been allowed to draw.

As a boy, Thomas spent a winter on the Limfjord (A big fjord in Northern Denmark) picking up his fishing nets before the water froze. A thin ice had formed, making it difficult to maneuver his little dinghy. At one point, the ice caused the boat to tip over and Thomas fell into the icy water. He struggled for a long time but could not get up on his own. His heavy clothes pulled him deeper into the water.

He tried to crawl into the shore. According to Thomas, he could feel his body slowly losing control. First, the fingers, arms, and slowly the rest of his body stopped functioning. Eventually he could no longer feel the cold and he just got more and more tired. Once he had entered very shallow water, he could only use his elbows, so he used them to keep his head above water.

Fortunately, he was discovered by some farmers in their field down by the fjord. They saw the lifeless body lying in the water and were fortunately able to pull him out.

He was carried up to a farm nearby and was laid on the dining table. His lifeless body was completely still, and everyone was sure he was dead, so they did not try to revive him. The doctor came quickly and declared Thomas dead. Thomas could hear this and tried to speak but his mouth wouldn't make any words.

Luckily, one of the men saw that Thomas' one finger was moving a little. He shouted, "He is still alive" and then they all started working frantically. They started warming him up with blankets. Slowly he came back to life.

According to Thomas, "dying" was not unpleasant at all, but it was the waking up part that was the hardest to endure.

Thomas' father Lars was a fisherman on the Limfjord all his life, so the family naturally spent a lot of time on the water. Already as a 12 - 13-year-old, Thomas got his own small boat and sailed all alone out on the open sea and up south of Læsø (An island between Denmark and Sweden) to fish. When he had caught enough, he sailed to Aalborg to sell the fish he had caught. For the money he earned there, he bought some other fish in Aalborg, which he knew would make him some more profit if he sailed on to Nibe and sold them. When all the fish were sold, he sailed back to Læsø.

All of this took place in a very tiny wooden boat of about 5 feet, with a very small cabin. Part of the trip involved navigating the open sea. It probably took about two days just to get to Læsø. The waves could be very imposing. For many years this little boat was at the harbor at Gjøl - and it was inconceivable to think that Thomas could live in this modest little boat. But still, he looked back on this as one of the best times of his life.

Later he was apprenticed as a bricklayer - mostly because that's what his big brother Carl Ejner did. Since Thomas has always had a very skinny body, that line of work did not suit him. The cold, the heavy stones, and the cement buckets were too much for his frail little body.

So, he instead found an apprenticeship as a baker, probably because it was warmer inside the bakery.

He cheated with his apprenticeship, because after three years he traveled to Copenhagen and declared himself finished. There he got a job in a patisserie where he had to make *kransekager*, (A danish cake made of Marzipan) among other things. Shortly after, the pastry chef discovered that Thomas made amazingly beautiful figures. Soon he was only making *kransekage* figures because the customers loved them so much. Eventually he grew tired of this and wanted to move on to something else.

The pastry chef cried when he left because he lost the opportunity to have Thomas' fine figures on his cakes.

When Thomas stopped at the bakery, he didn't have any plans for the future. It was difficult to find a job at that time in Copenhagen, and eventually he ran out of money. But Thomas was determined that he would not come crawling back to Gjøl. So, he had to come up with something in a hurry.

He got an idea to go out to Hellerup (North of Copenhagen), to the rich people who lived there and ask if they had any clothes that they would donate to him, because he had nothing. They usually felt sorry for the frail little man standing outside the door in his worn-out clothes, so they often complied.

Then he went to Copenhagen and sold the clothes he had just received. He would then put on his worn clothes again and return to Hellerup. He made quite a bit of income this way.

But the turning point came when he one day sat in the homeless shelter, eating with the other homeless people. He sat in his worn clothes ready to go to Hellerup.

There was an old vagabond who pushed his food over to him and said "Take this - you probably need it more than me."

That was the tipping point for Thomas. "I can't go on like this", he though. He bought some new clothes and went back to Gjøl.

In the late 1930's, he built his own bakery in Gjøl. But the thirties were very difficult times and people simply had no money to spare.

He drove around in his old car and tried to sell bread to the farms, but they could not pay. When World War II came, he had to close his bakery.

He tried a work shoveling snow but again, Thomas' frail body made this difficult. So, he began to whittle wooden figures and sell them. This was a more successful endeavor than the bakery and he found many customers.

Thomas took his bike and rode around and found some of the few people who had money at the time: doctors, priests, teachers and the like. Finally, his little family could make a living from it.

He later began making larger figures. One of the first was a large elephant with a man sitting inside cycling, making it look like it was walking. It was ordered for the amusement park in Aalborg.

In 1947, Thomas' brother returned home from the United States for a visit and Thomas traveled with him back to learn new things. There he learned, among other things, to cast with natural rubber, and could see that it could be the perfect material for his large figures.

When he got home, he started making large figures for the amusement park and for shop displays.

One of the largest figures he made was of the giant troll Uras. It could move and was used in markets around the country. He was really proud of this giant figure.

Uras was bought by a truck driver that delivered to the country markets. Poor Uras, however, didn't live very long. He was killed one day the trucker had put him up on the bed of his truck and was driving under a bridge without thinking about Uras' height. Uras could not be repaired and had to be laid in the ground.

LAJLA DAMS STORY

For many years, my mother Lajla's story has been neglected and forgotten. Mostly because her brother Niels Dam has a very hard time accepting the large part, she played in the Trolls' becoming what they are today. Therefore, I think Lajla herself should be allowed to tell things as they actually happened back then. This was before my time.

Here is her story, told by Lajla herself:

> When I was 14-15 years old, I helped my father Thomas Dam make figures for ghost trains. Later we made large gnomes for the shops that were 2.5 meters tall, where a person could sit inside and move the eyes, mouth, and arms.
>
> These large figures were sold to Denmark, Norway and Sweden. Some were even sold to

Germany. Unfortunately, it was a very seasonal job, so there were periods when there was not much to do.

At one point, a decorating company wanted my dad to make some little christmas gnomes, but in my dad's opinion, they wanted too much control over what they would look like, so the project ran out of steam. He would never compromise on the uniquely positive expressions that he created.

At about the same time, a man arrived who wanted us to make figurines as prizes for his raffle at the amusement park and at markets. He wanted us to make heads, hands and feet for these dolls. Dad asked if it was something I would like to try.

He first modeled in clay, and a plaster mold was made that the rubber model could be cast in. At that time, everything was made of natural rubber *with some red color mixed in to represent the skin tone.*

I earned some really good pocket money, and I even had a girl that helped me. These were the small beginnings of a troll factory.

Unfortunately, this business venture stopped abruptly when the man could not pay. Therefore, we decided to make the whole troll ourselves. It had turned out that we could sell them well so I wanted to continue.

The hair was made from small pieces of fur which we sewed together into a whole wig. The clothes were made of felt with holes and patches to make it look old. As you probably know, Trolls never wear new clothes.

The first eyes for the trolls were made by a dental technician who also made artificial eyes for humans. Later we found out the trolls looked best with brown teddy bear eyes. They were more friendly.

Meanwhile, I turned 17 and wanted to expand the business by going on the road and selling the trolls.

The first place I visited was a large store in Copenhagen called Havemanns Magasin.

Dad had previously sold a large christmas figure to them that reached from one floor to the next. There was a roller coaster inside it. It started in one arm and went down to the next floor.

I thought they knew what kind of things we were doing so it would be a good place to start. The head of the toy department was very friendly and accommodating, but he had a list of changes we should make to the trolls before they were ready to be sold.

I took a bit of offense at this and went home again and continued to make the trolls OUR way.

We made several different troll models and little by little they started to look like they do today.

The first many trolls were sold to friends, and friends of friends. We earned money to buy materials with.

My father Thomas at first did not take the small trolls seriously. He said to me "Lajla, these little trolls are bad business. I can get DKK 15,000 for a large troll and you only get DKK 15.00 apiece for the small trolls." (The monthly salary in 1958 for a worker was then around DKK 1,000).

One day an acquaintance came to see Dad and visited us. He saw the trolls I was sitting and making. Most of the work of making the trolls took place in our small living room. He got very excited about the little trolls, and said he was sure they would be a huge success.

He knew two American businessmen who were visiting Denmark. One was an expert in production and the other worked in PR and marketing. They could also see something special in the trolls.

During this time, my father built a new workshop in the middle of Gjøl to be able to make the large figures. Previously, it had taken place in a German bunker from World War II. Very safe - but not very practical.

This workshop was quickly redesigned to handle the production of the little trolls instead, and more and more employees soon arrived.

My mother Betty had a mink farm which was doing really well, but it was sold to make money to build the new factory and the machines for it.

MY TROLL LIFE

A journalist came by to do an article on the trolls, and I was on the front page with my arms full of trolls. It was Familie Journalen, which at this time was one of Denmark's largest magazines.

Then it really took off and shops from all over the country called and bought trolls.

For the first many years, there was no need for salespeople. The trolls sold themselves. The trolls were sent COD by mail. My little VW made lots of trips to the local post office often several times a day.

Our accounting at the time consisted of a small filing box with handwritten notes. So it was all very simple and straightforward.

At this point, my dad could see there was a lot more business in making lots of little trolls - not large ones.

Jep Andre Laponnel

During those years we grew more and more busy with the trolls and the small troll factory was expanded many times including the addition of an apartment we lived in.

A HAPPY BOY WITH HIS TROLLS

It was early morning on Friday the 27th of April, 1962 in the small town of Gjøl north of the Limfjord. The weather was good and the small town of Gjøl was waking up. The people who worked at the troll factory were on their way to work.

Lajla had another job that morning - namely giving birth to me - and she wanted to have it finished before the girls came to work. The apartment I was born in was connected to the factory and she did not want the girls to be able to hear her giving birth. So just a few minutes before 7 AM I was born.

So, you can safely say that I - literally - was born in the troll factory. Right at the start of the shift - one thing I have held on to for the rest of my life.

From then on, my whole life has been related to the trolls. From the first years and throughout my life.

My mom was only 21 years old when she got pregnant, and it was definitely not planned. It was the result of a short fling with a man from Aalborg, and not something she wanted to continue.

She has - as you have already read - always been a strong and independent woman, so she chose to raise me alone. At that time, however, it was mostly the norm to get married when a woman became pregnant - but my mother was never one to follow the norm.

No matter what people in town said, she did what she pleased, also this time around. She said she was better able to handle this by herself and since she made good money on the trolls, it was not a problem.

Grandma and grandpa said they should probably support her and they certainly did. My dad was put on my birth papers, but he didn't have to pay anything or assume any other responsibilities.

Unfortunately, I never met my father, but after his death in 2004, I met his two beautiful daughters, Anett and Helle -

and we have a very close relationship. And through them I have gained a good knowledge of my father.

I never felt like a father was missing in my life though. I had Grandpa in that role. I was often asked if I wanted to look for my father - and I might have - but I would always put it off. I probably also figured that it should be one's father who would try to get in touch and not the child. But there are arguments for both sides.

I later found out through my two half-sisters, that my father had had a secret closet in his apartment, which they were told they should not touch under any circumstances. Over the years, he had collected a lot of newspaper clippings of articles featuring me in connection with the trolls. It was really touching to hear - and I thought "Why didn't you contact me if you were so interested in me?". But I wasn't angry or resentful. I think he probably wanted to, but he didn't dare because he had misunderstood Grandpa saying that they would take care of me and that he didn't have to participate.

My grandfather always gained a lot of inspiration from the people he met. Having a new baby around of course greatly inspired him in his work with dolls.

I was the model for the very first doll in clay, both the larger doll and the very small 8 cm baby trolls. A rather special way to be immortalized.

It was something completely different from the trolls that we were used to. I would say that this was fortunate, as I don't think I look like a troll. However, it still had Thomas' typical expression, with the big warm eyes and smile. It was a doll with moving arms; a girl and boy doll in light, mulatto, and dark. So, at a very early age I was able to identify with both sexes, and all skin tones.

The dolls were produced for many years and become a popular collector's item for troll collectors.

It's a really cute doll, so I take that as a compliment that I must have been a cute baby. Or maybe it was Grandpa's love that did it. I will let you be the judge.

LIFE WITH GRANDPA – THOMAS DAM

Since I had never known my father, Thomas was, as I said, a kind of father figure to me. Mother and I lived in an apartment attached to the troll factory, with a door leading into the production area. Therefore the trolls were a big part of our lives.

My grandfather and grandmother Thomas and Betty also lived in a house adjacent to the factory, so there was plenty of contact, almost every single day.

Grandpa was an incredibly productive man throughout his life and can hardly remember a day he did not work. He simply couldn't help it. All the characters, drawings, and stories that were in his head just had to come out somehow. For him, it was not work at all. It was something he could not hold back.

We always had lots of fun and my whole childhood was filled with trolls and exciting stories.

His workshop was in the factory, and as a boy I was very much together with Grandpa. When I came out to him at his workshop, we always had fun talking. He always sat and worked at the same time, and most often he gave me a lump of clay, a piece of wood, or something else to make figures with. I was not supposed to sit empty handed while we were talking.

He had the ability to tell an exciting story totally out of the blue. He created adventures completely spontaneously and a story would develop out of it. There were stories about magic trolls, mice, little men on the moon and so on.

Most of the time, I was able to decide for myself what the adventure would be about. I came up with something, and then we would go on an exciting journey into a magical fantasy world.

One of the stories I enjoyed the most was the one about the little mice that lived with a little troll. They all lived in a mailbox. They had previously lived in a small farmhouse, but it had unfortunately burned down, so they had moved out into the mailbox. It was more cramped than in the house, but they were still comfortable.

One day, a mail order catalog with toys was delivered into the mailbox. In the catalog there were lots of things they could use, but they didn't know how to go about buying them.

That's not a problem, said the little troll. I have a purse and every time I open it there is a new gold coin in it. So, we can just buy whatever you want. All you need to do is choose,

It is a dream scenario for a little boy to be able to get all the toys he could hope for. So, I let my imagination go.

The game was then that I had to decide each time what they bought, and then Grandpa spun an adventure around it.

One day it might have been about a toy train that they bought so they could all more easily pick up nuts in the woods. Another time, they bought a toy plane so they could see everything from above. And how the plane was about to lose control because the troll was a little too wild and flew too fast.

They bought toy cars and drove on excursions, and toy boats so they could sail on Sundays on the small lake next to the house.

The topics seemed endless and the stories always created lots of beautiful images in my head.

Grandpa was not only good at making figures, but he could also draw the most amazing drawings. He and I drew together very often, and he always tried to motivate me to draw every day. We had a lot of fun with those drawings.

One of our favorite pastimes was drawing "Fjøkker". Of course, a name my grandfather invented.

In Gjøl - which was once an island - there are two parts on the north side. Østerkær and Vesterkær. Between them lies Nørredige. And it was at Nørredige that "Fjøkkerne" would battle each other.

The "fjøkker" were some huge monsters and they lived in two groups. One in Østerkær and another in Vesterkær. They had previously been a family, but now they had become enemies. None of them could remember why but fight they would.

We each chose who we would be, and then the war started. We each drew a monster - and sometimes it got out of hand with those monsters.

Grandpa first drew a monster, and then I drew one that attacked it. Then he drew a monster that attacked my monster, and then I had to defend myself with an even worse monster.

It required a large piece of paper, as you can imagine. Sometimes my grandmother had to break in to calm us down a bit - and say "Thomas - you must not teach him things like that". Then we giggled a bit and behaved - but only for 10 minutes. Then it got crazy again.

Grandpa once drew a man who was in the zoo and an elephant pooped in his pants. His suspenders could barely hold his pants up. My grandmother had to step in and stop the game. That's enough, you two. And we could not draw more that day.

MY FIRST JOB AT THE FACTORY

Right from the start, I was interested in everything that was going on at the factory. Especially my grandfather's work. Once, when I was about 5 years old, I was standing and looking at my grandfather while he was making natural rubber figures for molds. I asked "Grandpa - have you peed in it". This natural rubber had such a characteristically sharp smell. My grandfather laughed so much that he had to stop work.

There was always something exciting going on in his company, so I followed everything with intense interest. I must have been 6-7 years old when I said to him one day with great conviction: "One day I will probably come and run the factory for you grandpa".

He probably did not take it very seriously at the time, but he told me about the situation several times later, when we talked about it. "You knew very early on what you wanted, and you were right," he said.

So yes - my plan for the future was very clear early on. And I realized that was what I wanted in my life.

Living in a troll factory was like living in a fantasy land for a boy. There were lots of exciting places. We could race around on the office chairs, play hide and seek, or just run around. I know it was not a huge factory, but in my boyhood, it was a huge place.

During the Christmas holidays we could set up our giant racetrack in the production area and spend lots of hours there. So, the longer the Christmas holidays - the happier we were.

Grandpa has always worked very hard all his life, and he also quickly taught me that I should work if I wanted something.

I worked in the factory to earn pocket money. One of the first things I did was assemble cardboard boxes for the dolls that were made in my image. It was a good job - but I cut myself a lot on the boxes. But I persevered and earned my pocket money every month.

I was certainly not very fond of school. In fact, I hated it more than anything else. Mainly because I was bullied a lot because I was quite different. I had longer hair and wore very different clothes. And the fact that my family had the city's largest workplace also made me a favorite victim of bullying.

Another thing that made me so tired of school was that time seemed to move so slowly during classes. I got really bored in class during school hours.

I was absent from school a lot, and eventually mom made the decision to stop everything. We got approval so I could drop out of school in 8th grade. What a huge relief that was and I was really able to enjoy life again.

However, it didn't give me a lot of freedom since I started to work full time at the factory. But that work suited me perfectly.

I did lots of different things - from cutting the edges of the cast trolls, to putting eyes in, gluing hair on, and packing them in plastic bags.

Later on I started packing orders, and sending them out to the stores. We initially had a courier bike that we could ride to the post office with. Sometimes the little post office would be completely crammed with boxes, and they asked if we could come with the rest tomorrow.

Later I got to work at the plastic foundry. It was difficult, hot work with the over 200 degree molds that were cooled down in water and sent a cloud of hot steam up into my face. But I made good money and got lots of exercise.

The other men who worked in the foundry, for example Arne Svendsen, and Egon, were really fun to work with. Lots of Jutlandic dialect. Dry, sarcastic jokes flew through the air all day long, mixed with the noise of the machines and steaming water. It made the hot, hard work a lot easier.

The plastic foundry had windows facing the local convenience store - and almost without exception, the people who went into the store got some comment along the way.

I have heard that many people first went to the convenience store to shop after we had stopped at the troll factory, precisely to avoid the comments that they certainly got along the way. The comments, however, were never vicious, but really funny. But it's possible that not everyone would agree.

Already early in that period, my uncle Niels can see how efficient I am, and he is constantly very jealous. He tries to limit me in every way and keep me from working. But all his attempts just make me more and more determined.

I think it's ridiculous that he does it because any success I have means a success for the entire operation. It's also his win if all goes well but he doesn't agree.

But - resistance causes motivation so it just got me to work even harder.

My uncle has never been a particularly stable worker in the factory. He came in late during the day, making sure also to get off early. We joked that he was afraid of being locked inside the factory.

Over the years, my mother and I have always worked very hard at the factory - but there is also a strange principle that when I work, my mother and my salary must be seen as one. Niels should then have the same salary as the two of us together. So double salary. Jeppe and Lajla are family - was the explanation.

Niels' girlfriend also worked at the factory but oddly enough, the same does not apply to them because they are not related. They live together, but it's not the same.

A good example of some bizarre logic at the factory. There will be lots more examples later in the book.

But despite the oddness, I love my job at the factory, and like to seize any opportunities that come my way. Or rather, I create my own possibilities. And that's probably what has caused my uncle's hatred so much.

At the factory, most of the people working there were locals and mostly women. The loyalty and responsibility they showed towards the factory and for their work was completely unique. Sick leave was very low, and they occasionally came to work with a fever so others wouldn't need to bear the burden of working without them. But I also know that during all these years we have taken good care of them all.

Gjøl is a very small town with about 1000 inhabitants in the north of Denmark. At that time a lot smaller. In a small community like this, there is usually a great deal of interest in everything that is going on. The troll factory definitely functioned as a kind of newsroom throughout the years where information was exchanged on a grand scale.

The sound of the voices drowned out the sound of exhaust systems and sewing machines. But the atmosphere was good and there were lots of laughs.

Some will say it's just gossip but I see it more as an interest in each other. Because if there is one thing you experience in Gjøl, it is the fantastic care and support for each other. Both then - and fortunately still to this day.

Sometimes the talking got very loud, and one day Thomas said that he would go in and see if all those hens had laid eggs because of the clucking.

Thomas was always very humble and down to earth, and regardless of whether or not he was an incredibly talented artist, he certainly did not let it go to his head. He always wanted to help, and there were very frequent visits to his workshop with people who wanted to talk.

One funny event took place when one day a truck with plastic came to the factory. Thomas came in his work clothes to help empty the truck, just like the rest of us. The driver saw some trolls in a box and asked if he could have one. Grandpa said yes, he could. The driver did not know he was talking to the owner, so he asked what the boss would say to that. Thomas said "I don't think he will say anything about it. He probably thinks it's all right".

Thomas never wanted a big deal made out of him. He didn't want to be called director. It sounded too fancy, he thought, so he called himself a manufacturer instead.

THE AMERICAN

After the great success with the trolls in 60's, the sale of the trolls went on quite quietly for several years - and things were going ok. The trolls were sold around Denmark, and there were a bit export to Norway and Sweden as well. But no really big orders - and there are also several financially difficult times for the factory.

In 1982, an American businessman traveled through Kastrup Airport, after attending some meetings in the Far East. He was in a really bad mood because those meetings had not gone very well.

He walks around angrily waiting impatiently for his plane on to New York.

As he stomps around, he goes past a gift shop, and sees a little troll looking up at him with kind eyes and a big smile.

He can't help but look at it, and suddenly he notices that his bad mood is gone and that he is actually standing there laughing. He immediately walks into the store and buys the troll.

He looks again at the little troll several times during the plane ride home, and each time he feels happy.

When he gets home, he cannot help but think that if this little troll can change his mood so quickly, then it will also be able to do the same with others.

He finds out where the factory is located and sends us a letter requesting a collaboration. This was long before emails, so correspondence was somewhat slower.

I am at this point 20-21 years old and see his letter lying unanswered for some time in the office. I ask if I can reply to this letter because I'm probably better at English, and I also think it's really exciting.

When I think back on how amateurish this letter I sent was, it amazes me that the American wrote back in the first place. It was poorly composed and probably had some serious grammatical errors.

But he responded nicely back quickly. I do not know what first impression he had - but it worked. We wrote a bit back and forth and talked on the phone. Before long, he was on his way to Denmark again, and came and visited the factory.

It became a landmark event for the troll factory, and it began a revival of the trolls in every way.

The trolls came to be called Norfin in the United States. It was a name put together from "Nordic" and "Orphan". The slogan was "Adopt a Norfin".

In the beginning, we weren't crazy about that name, but we still accepted it. Until then, the trolls had been called Good Luck Trolls, and that was what they had become known as in the 60's. But we agreed to it and the strategy worked really well.

Sales got underway quickly and the orders coming from the USA just got bigger and bigger. The office was expanded with a fax machine. This was certainly something that Thomas considered some modern nonsense but I argued stubbornly. That fax also proved to be a good investment very quickly. It became the trolls' first step into a modern world.

My area of responsibility changed a lot, and I was responsible for most of the contact with the USA, and at the same time I took care of my work of packing the large orders - and the smaller orders that still came from Denmark, Norway and Sweden.

I was taught to make export papers and to work more with an administration mindset, together with Aase who was in the office as an accountant.

My mother was great at motivating me and never setting limits. She always said, "I KNOW you can do it if you want". It is a lesson that has certainly helped me throughout my life; how to achieve success even though there was plenty of resistance.

It was always a problem to keep up with the orders, and when they had to be packed, the small warehouse was too small. The many pallets of trolls had to be placed outside as they were packed.

THE NEW FACTORY

Eventually we realized that the old factory was no longer working. There was simply not enough space to produce all the trolls we were selling. We simply had to come up with something to solve the problem.

With the space problems we experienced at the factory, it was no longer justifiable, also in terms of work safety, to stay in the old factory. It was too cramped - and we were aware of that. The Labor Inspectorate later told me that they deliberately did not visit us because then they would be forced to reprimand us. So thank you for moving, they said.

Fortunately, a new industrial area in Gjøl had recently been established, and we bought one of the first plots there. And this plot had room for extensions which we also needed later.

Because we created lots of new jobs, we received regional development and business development support from EU funds. We also had consultants to help us create the most optimal production layout. It all helped us a lot to make a really effective factory.

Unfortunately, construction was quite delayed due to the support beams tipping over during assembly and all walls being pushed outwards. One carpenter got a flight he didn't ask for - but no one was injured. Only a few bruises, and a huge scare.

The new factory was finally completed in 1986, and on May 16, 1986, a large reception was held where almost the entire city participated.

The new conditions made everyone's work easier. Finally, there was room for a better production flow, and we had enough space to be able to have a larger stock of trolls. The packing of pallets with trolls was also no longer like playing Tetris.

In this new beautiful factory we had a completely new environment to increase sales and the production of the trolls. And increase sales we certainly did.

The line of new trolls expanded to many more sizes, and more clothing models each year. Previously, the range of different models and sizes had been quite limited. But in the coming years, we continuously developed new models.

Fortunately, Thomas had been very productive all his life, so there are plenty of faces and sizes to choose from when making a new line.

The ideas for the clothes come mostly in collaboration with my mother Lajla. Almost all the clothes for the trolls are designed by her.

During the same period, we started attending fairs all around, and I remember the first fair in Herning, where I attended alone. It was called Formland and was a place where buyers and shops from many countries came to shop twice a year.

I suggested we go and try this show out, and I said I could go alone. We made some plywood boxes - painted them white - and like (troll) magic, we had a trade fair stand. Some signs were made, and some pictures for the walls. Not the most creative trade show stand - but it worked as intended.

The first few times I spent the whole 5 days alone and I had a small sign with "Coming soon" if I had to go to the toilet. When I got back, the customers were standing nicely waiting. The amount of caramels I had available on the stand had gone down quite a bit, so the wait was probably ok.

Tom's Gold Caramels became a regular feature at the fairs and several kilos of it were always consumed. There were probably also a lot of toots fillings that got taken with them.

I have always followed the principle of getting started first and then learning how to do it perfectly along the way. If you wait for everything to be perfect, you will never get started. Better make a soapbox car and get started and then let it develop into a Ferrari slowly. That was also how we got started with the fairs. Then we continued to make them better and better along the way.

It was successful to attend the fairs and I ended up attending this fair over 30 times.

Every year we got a bigger and bigger stand, and it became much more creative. And luckily, we also got more help.

Later we hired a salesman for Denmark, Jesper, who was my ex-wife's brother. He is a phenomenal salesman, and he did a great job in Denmark. The fairs were even more fun because he was there.

TOO MANY TROLL COPIES

During these years, countless copies of the trolls appeared and unfortunately, we could not do much about it.

In the 60's a number of trolls had been sold in the USA, without copyright notice on them, so the rights had unfortunately been lost.

Despite the many copies - which were usually a bad quality - the original trolls sold really well - maybe even better than they would have if so, much attention had not been generated from the copies.

I remember one year I was at the big toy fair in Nuremberg, Germany. At this time, it was the center of all toy trade. At this fair alone, I counted about 36 companies that sold copies of the trolls. It was mostly Chinese companies, and with very varying quality. There have probably been many more copies, but I got tired of counting.

We tried to find ways to stop them - but each time we hit a wall.

Thomas was also against this legal action. He was certainly not much for having to file lawsuits to enforce his rights either. He went through some lawsuits during the first troll wave in the 60's and he was really tired of it.

He had had several very bad experiences with being in court. He hated all the lies that were told during such trials. He once won a lawsuit in the United States, and the man who had copied the trolls went out after the trial and shot himself. Thomas never quite got over it.

Another thing we considered, weighed up against the bad odds we had in the lawsuits, was that we simply could not produce more than we did. So the idea was that we shouldn't spend a lot of energy and money on something that would not really change our situation.

The troll crazy also got other types of attention. I remember one day we were called up by one of the competitors from the USA, who made the most copies. It was Russ Berrie who was a very large company who made many different things to the gift business. They had a large collection of troll copies.

It was the company president calling and I picked up the phone. He said:" Hey, we wanna buy your company. Let's talk ". He went straight to the point.

Of course it was flattering but my grandfather quickly said "That asshole Russ who has been copying us for so many years should not have the company, no matter what they want to pay", and the whole family agreed. So it was a short meeting and Russ got an answer back, though without hearing Thomas' exact words.

Several years later, the laws were changed in the United States and it became possible to restore the artist's rights and fortunately that stopped most copies.

THOMAS LEAVE THIS WORLD

On the evening of November 12, 1989, my grandfather died after a long battle with cancer. It was the evening before mom´s birthday.

We had many good talks during his illness but when I held his hand and he took the very last breath that November evening, there were still things I had not talked enough about, I think. But by then it was too late. Such a strange feeling. An era was coming to an end. What silence and emptiness I felt. It took a really long time to get over his death.

He had said several times during that period, "Now that I'm dying, do not throw Niels out. I know he does not want to work but take care of him now."

I promised that and said we have always done that. I certainly could not see any reason to throw him out. He was annoying with all his grumbling and laziness, but we could never throw him out.

I also remember my grandfather saying it was ok to leave now. "I have experienced much more than most people experience in several lives". He had been incredibly productive all his life, traveling to many exciting places in the world so he could leave with a clear conscience.

Thomas had never been the least bit spiritual, but during his illness, things changed somewhat. He had several periods where he lost consciousness. When he woke up after that, he said that he could see his friends who were already dead, standing over on the other side and waiting for him.

"It's like a threshold I just have to walk over before I can get over there," he said. "They are standing there on the other side waiting. Sløk the art dealer, Hertzberg and all the other assholes. Peace after death - I don't believe in it. Not when they are all there", he said with a tired laugh. He was quite ready to leave.

After my grandfather's death, my grandmother Betty Dam took over the title of director of the company - mostly pro forma, because in reality I was the one who ran the company. She certainly did not want to take on the managerial and administrative responsibility of running a growing business.

After some time, however, we agree that it is more logical if I am the director of the company. It had probably been most natural if it was my mother or my uncle Niels who took over.

My mother immediately said that she was not interested in taking that responsibility, and Niels clearly showed with his work effort and lack of insight into running a business that it was certainly not a workable solution that he became director.

A NEW TROLL IS BORN AT THE TROLL FACTORY

A year after my grandfather's death, a new troll was born: my daughter Martine. At that time, we live in a small apartment that used to house the troll production.

There was not much time for maternity leave, so we went back to work very quickly - and of course Martine was there with us. She didn't go to daycare. It went well and we enjoyed having her with us all the time. She was an easy child, so we could easily work while she lay asleep, or played on the floor beside us. Her grandmother was there too, so it worked well.

5 years later, Josefine was born and she also came to work with us for some time.

The two girls got their introduction into the troll world just as I had. Unfortunately, they weren't able to be immersed in it as much as I was.

A SMALL TROLL TEAM

Despite things moving so fast, we were a small administration team: my mother Lajla Dam who also owned 40% of the company, my then wife Mette, a secretary, and myself as director.

We all took care of many different tasks.

In addition to being a director, salesman, and the one who traveled, when necessary, I packed orders when needed along with the others. We all helped to empty containers when trolls produced in the Far East arrived. There was no excuse for lazily sitting in the office when there was real work to do.

There was always a great sense of togetherness at the factory, and as always lots of chatting in production. The employees always had a great sense of responsibility, which had characterized the troll factory all these years.

We also did everything we could so that they would be comfortable and flexible.

In the years before 1986, when there was usually less turnover around Christmas, the girls in production had always been let go and sent home from the beginning of December until February / March every year. It suited them all really well, because then they could prepare for Christmas in peace.

When the factory got busier, however, this could no longer be done and they were quite angry about that. "Can't we even be fired anymore," they said. It was said with a wink, so they probably weren't being serious.

THE TROLLS TRAVELS THE WORLD

The number of countries where we sold the trolls continued to grow. I travelled a lot those days - to start up production and to visit our distributors all over Europe.

As a rule, I left early in the morning, and returned home again in the evening, so as not to lose time in the office. I also wanted to go home and be able to take my two girls to school in the morning.

This packed travel schedule worked for most countries in Europe. First flight from Aalborg in the morning, change in Copenhagen, and so out in Europe. A few hours meeting in London, Birmingham, Stockholm, Paris, Amsterdam, Frankfurt, or somewhere else. A little walk in the city after the meetings - and then back home again - with a flight change in Copenhagen again, and touch down in Aalborg again 23:30. Satisfied and tired and totally filled up with coffee and SAS's fantastic cookies.

Many times, it was a tough trip with three flights out in the morning and three flights home in the evening. I would come home totally burnt out by all that waiting time. However, I have always enjoyed the wait at an airport while watching people. There are always lots of stories about those people in my head, just like my grandfather always had.

My grandfather was like that. He loved to people watch and could fall completely into spells when out and about. Most of the times with his mouth open. Often my grandmother would have to tell him to close his mouth at least when he was looking.

In the period from 1990 to 1995, we sold over 10 million trolls annually. The larger troll models were mostly produced in Denmark, and all the smaller ones in China or Thailand. Most often, those who were going to the United States were sent directly from the factories in China - without us ever seeing them.

I clearly remember the day when we had to buy new calculators because the ones, we had did not have enough digits. I remember thinking how surreal that was.

All the trolls sold in England and in continental Europe came through the warehouse at Gjøl, and for several years in a row we received over a hundred 20 and 40 foot containers annually.

It was a huge logistical job to keep an eye on all the contracts, orders, and letters of credit (which we used at the time). When I think back, I can't imagine how we could handle it with the small staff in the office, but it worked.

There was fierce pressure all the time to get the orders produced in China on time. There were usually 30-60 days of production time at the factory. After that came 30-45 days of transport by ship. Then it all had to be repackaged and sent out again as soon as possible to the distributors who most often screamed and shouted at their trolls. As a rule, the trolls we received were sent out the same day to the distributors in Europe.

During the busiest period, we also sent quite a few of the trolls with air freight from China. It cost more - but luckily, we could afford it with our prices. Fortunately, we found a solution where they were sent by plane some of the way and then ship and road transport the rest of the way. That made it more affordable. And cuts the transport time down to less than half of ship transport and the price in half too.

I remember one night I was alone in the office and a message came about a big delay from one of our factories in China. It was a huge delivery, and we really needed those items. I got so angry that I kicked the office door.

This resulted in a very sore toe and a few weeks of being an invalid. I didn't tell anyone what had happened but said I had stubbed it on a wall. The kick didn't result in the delivery going any faster, so I never did it again. The door wasn't harmed from my rage.

To add to the challenges: during those years there were also EU quotas on the import of toys from China to Denmark and those quotas limited us very much. We had to predict sales months in advance, and that was almost impossible when we were growing so much. In addition, we could never get the quotas we wanted.

So those who say success comes easily should have been with us those years at the troll's factory.

THE NON EXCISTING MARKETING

At no time in all these years did we spend money on advertising and traditional marketing. It was also a long time before there was something called social media.

The fact that our story and the adventure of the trolls was told to the media was great for the trolls. That was the way it had gained momentum in the late 50's. And it has continued to do so throughout the years.

In England, we worked with a PR agency, and that meant that we had a large media presence throughout England. The trolls have an exciting story to tell, and they appeal to people so much. This works much better than ads.

In Denmark, we had so many articles written about us that would have cost a up to a million dollars if it had been ads. In England we got many times more exposure through articles and TV. People believe in articles much more than ads, so a good article is important for a product like the trolls. Actually, for any product.

I worked hard all the time to find importers and distributors, in as many countries as possible - mostly in Europe, but certainly other countries further away. I did not want us to be so dependent on only the United States and England. It was too dangerous to depend only on one, so I knew we needed to diversify. Just like we always had more than one factory in China for production. We didn't want to be caught with a broken supply channel if one of the factories had problems.

In England, Trolls had quickly become the latest fad, and almost all school children had to bring one or more trolls to school. They had the trolls lined up on the table, on pencils, school bags and everywhere else. But the trolls did not only appeal to school children. They appealed to people of all ages, so it was difficult to say who was buying them.

The music channel MTV, which was really big in those years, had Trolls as a fixed element in their studio for a long time, and it worked really well for sales as well. The hosts played with the trolls, and they were also featured in competitions.

Norway and Sweden have always been natural markets for the trolls, so they are almost considered our home market. They have the same culture with Trolls as we have in Denmark.

Germany and the Benelux were pretty hard to get started in, and it required lots of legwork and countless attempts. But finally, we found a Belgian agent who had good connections, and the big German, Belgian and Dutch department stores finally stocked the trolls.

I had learned to never give up. No matter how long it takes. If one way didn't work, then you tried another way. In the end, you will eventually find the solution. Too many give up at the first signs of resistance and that is a shame.

A MEETING OF CULTURES

My work during these years was constantly changing with the different cultures, and very different markets. It was a challenge, but it was also really exciting. No two countries have the same business culture and all need to be treated differently.

All from the way you dress at business meetings, to how much small talk was needed before speaking "business", and the way you would address someone.

With all that traveling to multiple countries in a week, I had to watch what I was saying. But I don't think I made any major mistakes.

A large Japanese department store chain also finally stocked the trolls after we had been trying to enter the Japanese market for 4-5 years. Finally, they said yes - and their buyer came and visited us while he was in Europe. It was a great pleasure to have a visit from the Japanese buyer.

One morning I picked him up at the hotel, he was sitting with bags under his eyes, and he looked really tired. I asked worriedly what had happened. I thought he had become ill.

But it was summer, and he had enjoyed so much sitting and looking out of his hotel room on the bright Danish summer night. He had never experienced that before, so he did not want to miss it.

The coffee flowed freely in huge quantities at our meeting afterwards. We became really good friends and I was even invited as a private guest with him in Japan. Unfortunately, I never had the time to do so. But it was a great honor and a sign of trust.

I have had so many amazing experiences with the trolls and my visits to distributors all over the world. We also always tried to give the visitors a good Danish experience.

I especially remember a buyer who visited us from Taiwan. When he arrived, he had seemed like a dry and very formal businessman. But during the day, you can guarantee that he thawed out a bit.

We talked about everything, and he told us about his life in Taipei. He said he loved to ride a mountain bike in the forests outside Taipei. I had trouble imagining a little round Chinese man in a tight cycling suit riding around in a forest. Fortunately, I was able to get that image out of my head and concentrate on our meeting again.

Of course, he also had to have a real Danish dining experience, so I took him to restaurant Fyrtøjet in Aalborg. At that time, they served really good traditional Danish food, and he loved it.

He loved the Danish food, and he ate a lot, and with normal Chinese politeness, he smacked his lips and burped a lot. In China, this is a sign that you really enjoy the food. The other guests at the tables next to us didn't seem to be enjoying his "politeness" as much as we were. They looked a little upset. But the most important thing was that he enjoyed it very much, so I did not bother saying anything to him.

Our American distributor Steven, who was by far our biggest customer, visited us at Gjøl many times, and he was also really happy with the Danish food. We always made sure he got some good Danish experiences to take home with him. Once we were at the local inn and had Danish open sandwiches for lunch. He was Jewish, and therefore could not eat pork.

My uncle said that now he should teach that little Jew a lesson and ordered some open sandwiches with pork. Steven didn't seem to know what it was, so he ate it - and Niels had a laugh afterwards, thinking he was really funny.

The rest of us felt bad about this stupid joke. We all thought it was a total lack of respect for the man who had actually helped us bring the trolls to life again. And total disrespect for other people's religion.

WE DOUBLE IN SIZE - YEAR AFTER YEAR

The turnover in the Troll Company more than doubled for several years in a row during that period. It's great to see things just grow and grow, and to see all the things you have worked so hard for, just succeed - across the board. And as you can see, it went almost too well.

It is an indescribable feeling when a small factory up in North Jutland can be known across the globe, and have such a positive impact on the people who buy its products.

The Trolls came in lots of hair colors, clothing styles, and lots of sizes. There were Christmas trolls, and Easter trolls too.

A big item in those years was also our Troligan troll in red and white colors, which was made in connection with

Denmark's participation in the Football World Cup and European Championships. It sold very well in the following years and it was even made in other countries' colors.

In 1992, we once again expanded the factory at Gjøl with twice as large a warehouse and a larger office. At the same time, we had rented another factory space at Gjøl, where 30-40 ladies sat and made trolls as well. So the little town was steaming of activity.

The staff are amazingly loyal and they always did go that extra mile when needed. This resulted in lots of overtime in production, but it was not enough to meet the demand.

We couldn't keep up with demand at all - no matter how hard we tried. I think we could have sold 3-4 times as much if we could have just produced them. Maybe even more.

The great success was at times also stretching us out financially. It sounds paradoxical, but when you grow so fast, things don't necessarily become easier.

We usually gave our customers 30 days credit, and at the same time we had to pay 30-60 days prior to raw materials for what was produced in Denmark, or even longer prior to the trolls produced in China. You can probably figure out that it requires a lot of capital when you grow so fast. We made good money on the trolls, but with that growth, it was not enough.

We went to our bank at the time, Bikuben, and asked for more credit. We had the orders, and just needed a small liquidity to be able to produce it. Our accounting figures were really good, but still we only got a small increase in credit, and a message that we could just say no to more orders.

I simply could not wrap my mind around the limited mindset the bank had.

When we later had improved liquidity, they started to offer more loans. Yes please - I only need an umbrella when it rains - not afterwards.

During those days, I worked all the time. From early morning to late evening. Heading home and picking up my daughters - eating and then leaving for work again.

We had a map in the office with a label on Siberia that said VACATION. In Danish you talk about "towns in Russia" when referring to something that would never happen, and the idea of a vacation certainly fit the bill.

At some point, however, we took the opportunity to travel a week to Cyprus with the girls. Our secretary Sandra called a few times, to ask about different things. Each time, I had to spend a few hours getting back into vacation mode.

So I said to her, "Sandra, you know what to do. You are welcome to make the decision yourself. I trust that you can."

"OK I will do that. Then I will only call you if the factory is on fire," she replied. My answer was "No - you better call the fire department. It will take me at least 5 hours to get home".

REALLY GOOD ECONOMY

The economy in the factory was really good all these years. We had a profit of around 30-40% for several years in a row. Quite unique for a production company.

We did this by running the factory at a minimum cost, and outsourcing part of the production to China, for example. It gave us a maximum credit rating of AAA at Dun & Bradstreet.

In addition to producing the trolls themselves in Gjøl and in China, we are also starting to make licensing agreements those years. A license agreement is a contract with other companies to use Troll images on their products. For this right, they then pay us between 7.5 and 15% of the turnover on these products.

It was pure income without doing a lot of work. We produced a Stylebook, which set rules for how they could use the trolls and what designs they could use.

We made up to 100 different licensing agreements using the trolls around the world. We had an English licensing agent who was really good at finding companies all over Europe. Our US distributor also created many licensing agreements.

Soon the trolls appeared on everything from bags, pencil cases, ice cream, mugs, clothes, shoes, candy and more. Even as ice-creams in Israel. A cartoon was also made featuring the trolls which was published in England, Germany and the Netherlands.

AWARD FOR FASTEST GROWING COMPANY IN DENMARK, 1993

In 1993, there was a competition called *Danmarks Vækstvirksomhed* (company with the most and fastest growth) - organized by what was formerly known as Unibank, and Børsens News Magazine. I saw the ad for the competition in Børsens News Magazine occasionally - and did not really have time - but still sent in our numbers.

Shortly after, I was called by an auditing firm who said we were at the top - very much at the top. They wanted to come and check that the numbers actually were correct.

They came up to the office the following week and checked that the numbers I had submitted were correct. At the same time, there was a long interview where they gained more insight into, for example, the number of employees and the growth of that. I did not think much about it and had certainly not imagined we could win.

It probably took a month – and then one day I was told that we had won - and won big. A little incomprehensible to us. But we were super proud. However, we had to keep it a secret for some time before the award ceremony was held in Copenhagen.

The award was presented by Danish politicians Anders Fog Rasmussen and Mogens Lykketoft. The event was really well attended by lots of journalists and businesspeople. A really nice day - with lots of interviews and interesting conversations.

It was a really heavy statuette and when Minister of the Interior Mogens Lykketoft had to hand it to me, he asked me to hurry up and take it. Otherwise he would drop it.

There were countless articles and TV features. And of course lots of advertising for the factory.

The news was in the newspapers already that morning, and I remember that at the airport in Aalborg before we had to fly to Copenhagen, there were a lot of people who recognized me and wanted to talk. They said it was unbelievable with such success so quickly - and I thought "You should only know how much we have worked for many years for this". A quick overnight success like that takes about 10-15 years I said.

Everyone at the factory was happy and proud - and of course it was celebrated.

AALBORG EUROPEAN OF THE YEAR

At almost the same time in 1993-1994, I was named Aalborg European of the Year - that is, the Aalborg / North Jutland resident who had done the most to make the area known in Europe. There was a nice reception in Aalborg Hall, and the award was presented by the mayor.

DANISH MARKETING AWARD

Half a year later we were called by Henrik Bøtcher Hansen, who in his time had started the company HBH - later OBH which sells a number of different electrical appliances.

He had a few years earlier founded the Danish Marketing Award. The award had been given the year before to former minister for foreign affairs Uffe Elleman Jensen, and the Danish Tourist Board.

Elleman received the award for his marketing of Denmark in his work as Minister of Foreign Affairs and for his great work in the EU to get the Baltic countries Estonia, Latvia and Lithuania into the European Union.

We received the award for an unique marketing based only on PR both in Denmark and globally.

It was an exciting day in Copenhagen, with a reception hall full of guests and journalists.

Again, the award recipient was kept secret, so I was presented by marching into the hall after a small orchestra with trumpets and drums and marching band music. A royal entry.

I have to admit it did was a bit strange with this grand march and I felt a bit uncomfortable. It wasn't something I was used to coming from the little town of Gjøl.

But it went well and after a short presentation by Henrik Bøtcher Hansen it was my turn to give my speech. It went super well even though I felt my mouth was so dry it felt like it was filled with sand. But I received a lot of laughter and applause.

Afterwards, former Foreign Minister Uffe Ellemann-Jensen gave a nice speech for me. He told me that he actually knew my grandfather, and his wife Alice had grown up not far from Gjøl.

When Uffe Ellemann-Jensen was an ardent EU supporter, we had given him an EU troll in blue / yellow colors, and the star symbol on the shirt.

He used the troll in his speech and said he would take it to the Liberal European Parliament's parliamentary line-up meeting the following weekend. He thought the little troll would be a somewhat better candidate than the others lined up.

He repeated this line in an interview with the major newspaper Jyllands Posten the following week. I don't think the troll was voted in, but it was probably among the favorites.

We also received a prize of DKK 100,000 on a big check. Together with a small sculpture with the sun design.

After the award ceremony, it was really nice to sit and chat with Ellemann and his wife - former TV journalist Alice Vestergaard. Uffe is an incredibly witty man, and we had a fun afternoon with them.

Again the story appeared in several of the country's newspapers, and there were numerous interviews.

WHAT COMES UP...

At some point, troll sales were unfortunately starting to stagnate in several parts of the world. This is how it is with trends, and we had also been aware of that. It was definitely something we were expecting.

But the rapid slowdown in England, for example, was impossible to predict. In England that year, there were a few terrorist attacks that caused the retail trade to stop almost completely. People didn't dare to go out and shop anymore and that hit the retail industry hard.

We were caught with a pretty big stocks of trolls, which were actually already ordered by our distributor. But we didn't dare ship them because of their difficulty in paying. Better to keep them yourself - even if it causes problems with too much stock.

The economy was good enough, so we could manage, but we had to scale down production a lot - also in Denmark. Having to go lay off so many good and loyal people at the factory was really difficult. It was with a very heavy heart that I wrote and signed the dismissal papers for all the amazing employees.

At one point I traveled to Manchester to sell some of the trolls we had too many of, to an English company that specialized in surplus stocks.

I was picked up at the airport by a nicely dressed driver and a nice Bentley. I thought to myself "This is probably going to be good".

However, the truth came out when we were negotiating prices. I think we got a maximum of 50% of the cost price, or even less for the trolls we sold to them.

I would have rather been picked up in an old rusty Morris Minor - and then have gotten a better price.

At that point I can see it was necessary to diversify, and not just bet on the trolls. That's why we started selling a series of stuffed animals in good quality designed in the Netherlands. At this time, there were not many good stuffed animals on the Danish market, but I was sure that with the right products, it will probably be a success again.

The company designed a lot of good products, and also had a luxury series with WWF stuffed animals. These animals were rapidly doing very well in Denmark, and we are building up a large turnover on these animals very quickly.

Again here the sales went up fast, and at times it was difficult to get enough products to keep up with the demands - but we've gotten used to that.

WARNING

If you want to preserve the positive rose red image of the trolls and do not like drama, then stop reading here.

A CONSTANT BATTLE ON SEVERAL FRONTS

I would definitely have preferred to tell a beautiful story about the trolls, filled with harmony in a cozy family business in small town in Denmark. But if I have to tell the true story, then unfortunately there is a downside that must also be included; a very ugly side of the story.

Through all the years of lots of success there had been a jealous uncle. This was Thomas' son Niels who was 10 years younger than Lajla. So he was a very small boy in the years Thomas and Lajla began the troll production.

All the time I recall, he has created problems and stupid conflicts in the family. The first young years he was driving his mother and father, Thomas and Betty, crazy with his way of life. There were constant parties with lots of drugs and alcohol, and lots of noise from his apartment. He had some suspicious friends and the police were almost regular guests. Either to look for drugs, find any of his friends who were on the run from prison.

As a boy, I experienced the police with dogs suddenly entered the house while we sat and had breakfast. We lived in the apartment next door and they had come to the wrong place.

During my time at the factory, there were constant attacks and it just got worse and worse. So in addition to fighting to run the factory, sell and market the trolls, I also had to deal with the internal attacks that constantly came from my uncle.

I cannot count how many times the family had long talks to try to solve the problem. Especially with my granddad Thomas.

As a boy, I quickly came to know the sweet scent of marijuana in his apartment. And I was used to the sight of him and his friends totally stoned, almost unable to speak.

When things really took off I really felt - and we all did in the office - that we had to fight on two fronts all the time.

On the one hand, we had to sell products, develop and get everything produced. And on the other, we had to deal with this constant, and in my opinion completely meaningless, stupid internal struggle.

Niels was well aware that he could not run the factory. He clearly did not have the abilities and had never really shown much interest in it either. But at the same time, he was incredibly bitter about it, and it was primarily going to affect me. I was seen as the biggest threat.

Many times I was thinking about how much more we could have achieved with the troll factory if we had stood together and supported each other. Instead of foolish resistance because of jealousy.

My uncle is not, to put it mildly, the most industrious man in the world. He never has been. No matter how busy we were, he usually showed up at the factory in the late morning, and usually left quickly.

He often said that a good owner makes himself redundant by delegating. And he certainly perfected that. However, he didn't fully understand this.

Despite the good salary, nice car and free housing, we could never count on him as a stable worker. Friday, and often Thursday as well, was usually also a day off for him. He had no problem showing up the local bar though. But it was really good for the rest of us. Then we had peace of mind those days and didn't have to deal with his complaining and negative energy.

However, he took care of the production of molds and the operation of the plastic foundry. But ALWAYS with very long delays. If we asked him for help, the answer was "he was not our servant".

But he was part of the family and we accepted it.

I tried to smooth over the relationship with him and hold regular orientation meetings with him. Just so he was clued into what's going on. He was, after all, one of the owners, along with my mom.

Mom was at the factory every single day, from morning to night, and she knew everything that was going on. He was basically never there, so without these meetings with me, he would not have known anything at all about what was going on.

After these meetings, he usually quickly left the factory again, to immediately drive down to the bar in Gjøl, and brag about everything that "he" has taken care of in the company. The local friends were wildly impressed with how talented Niels is.

That was good enough for me. If only it made him feel better and act nicer, then that worked for me.

At times when we are really busy, however, it became too stressful to never know if we had his help or not. There were many delays during these very busy periods when he did not do the things that were agreed beforehand. We simply could not wait for him. The things that we agreed upon had to be done immediately otherwise the whole operation would shut down. A factory is a system of lots of moving parts and if one is not working - the whole system shuts down.

So I end up one day suggesting that he should only be the factory whenever he wants. He would still get his salary and all the perks, but that we would no longer expect his help.

That way we could plan differently, and I would no longer depend on him for anything. I told him he was obviously very annoyed whenever we asked him to help, so to avoid more conflicts it was better this way.

He agreed that it was probably for the best and he seemed relieved. But afterwards, as usual, he was ranting and raving over the very thing he had agreed to.

Often times I went to the factory evenings and weekends and packed orders. Niels would come by and say, "Wow, you're packing now?" Never an offer to help. He took a couple of boxes of trolls, which he needed to sell at the inn and then he was gone again. No offer to help or anything.

At a time when revenue had begun to stagnate, I said at a board meeting that we should think a lot about what we spent the money on. We had to invest wisely in new products such as the stuffed animals we sold with great success.

But shortly after, Niels had ordered a new BMW, and at the same time renovated his apartment for many hundreds of thousands.

THE COMPLAINING NEVER END

One summer I come up to the office on a Monday and there was a handwritten note with scrawled red lettering. It said something about me having to leave the board immediately because I had faked increased earnings on my and my wife's pay stubs.

Niels often spent a lot of time sitting in the office in the evenings and on weekends to check invoices and pay stubs. This would be something he could use against us. There he had seen an extra amount on our paycheck that month. It was about a few thousand kroner each, I think.

If he had asked, then he would have been told it was the holiday bonus that we all got and which he also got himself every single year.

As salaried employees, we did not receive holiday pay, but we did receive a 3% wage supplement, which then had to be paid in connection with holidays. In other words, a completely normal procedure. Of course, Niels also received this bonus.

He – once again - used the opportunity once again to create a conflict. I think he could see for himself - for once - how ridiculous it was.

In 1997, my then wife got pregnant again, but unfortunately the little boy was stillborn. A big shock to us because we had already seen him alive on scan and heard the heartbeat.

But unfortunately, he died of unknown causes during the pregnancy. It was so far into the pregnancy that it was almost like a real birth. We had an hour with the little boy so it was very emotional.

The next day I was back at work but was not really present. As usual, Niels was in a combative mood and yelled up about something silly. I said I had just lost a child and asked whether or not this discussion could wait. But his answer was "he did not care - the boy was our problem".

Niels had always insisted that he would be the one who traveled to China to talk to factories. He had good experience with the plastic foundry, so it made good sense.

The travels always were scheduled according to when he wanted to travel to Thailand and party. Not according to what was needed purely in terms of production. He certainly would not pay for the trip himself. He then took a few days in Hong Kong and China, and then spent a month in Thailand. Always at the company's expense, and of course with full pay.

When, after the meetings with the factories in China, he traveled to Thailand and partied for a month, he had of course totally forgotten what had been agreed upon when he returned home.

Therefore, each time I had to follow up directly with the factories and find out what was agreed during the meetings. It was embarrassing every time and we appeared incompetent.

When he finally came home, there was often an overview with an inventory of our purchases - with the bottom 5-6 cm torn off. We wondered why these statements were missing the bottom half. It was as if there was an extra calculation that we weren't allowed to see. He said it was how they did it in China. Later we found out why there were calculations that we were not allowed to see. A so-called over-invoicing was made. It happened when a price was made for the trolls we bought and then a percent was added to the price, which was invoiced officially. This overpayment was taken back outside of the company, or paid out on the next visit. He then tries to blame me for this but more on that later.

TAKING A BREAK

In 1997, I got completely burnt out from all the stress and conflict and I decide stop and seek new challenges. I decided to go back to school. I was really carried away by the foolish struggle in the company. We agree that I will return to the company after I have completed received my MBA. I say it's better that my mother and my uncle Niels run the business together and save my salary.

But that's not how it went at all.

Very soon after, mother is thrown out of the factory, which was her whole life and which she had created in collaboration with her father. One day Niels comes and tells her to leave the factory immediately. There's no need for her there anymore, so she should go right away. From one day to the next, she is kicked out of the troll factory she has spent her entire life in. Only because of one thing. In Niels' head, it is only he who has the rights to the trolls.

It was a very big mistake of mine to give him this opportunity. Knowing him I should have been able to anticipate this. But that he would throw out his own sister, was more than I expected.

To illustrate how small shoes he wear ill give you this example. One Lajla wanted to go pick up her toaster that was in the office. She called the secretary Sandra and told her that she would come and pick it up. Sandra said it was ok, but when she got up there, Sandra appeared embarrassed and said that Niels did not want her to have her toaster.

I stopped my education, and at the same time started my own business that went really well. We got an office in the old troll factory in Gjøl, which my mother had bought. In a very short time, we get a turnover of several million, with sales of, among other things, stuffed animals from England.

THE HUNT STARTS

Niels is well aware that he is not able to run the factory, so he gets help from a local friend, Calle Østergaard.

For several months, Niels and Calle Østergård had met almost daily at Niels' home to make plans and prepare their move, by forcing my mother and I out of the company.

I was later told that they had been running around the troll factory's office for several days, reviewing all the papers they could find to use against me - and cheering loudly when they found something they could use.

They then start their attack, mostly on me, but also my mother. In the beginning, we simply do not understand the meaning of it all. What's the point of all the things they are constantly attacking us with? Is it not enough that we are out of the factory?

They started by filing a bailiff case against me to stop my company from participating in the Formland fair in Herning. I remember I went and lined up in Herning without knowing if I would be stopped or not. But eventually I was told I could go on. The case was dropped.

Since that did not work, they immediately moved on to something else.

Then they tried to stop me using the marketing and competition law, saying I was not allowed to contact the same customers as them. I had not had an employment contract as a director and therefore there was no competition clause either. They said I had stolen their customer lists, but after all those years, I did not need a list to be able to remember the customers. They were all in my head since I had visited them many times. They also had to drop that case after a long legal discussion.

But they did not give up. They wanted to break us no matter what it took.

There was also a bailiff's case with things they said I had taken from the factory when I was employed there. They had made a list of 21 different things that they claimed I stole.

These were completely foolish things and I could hardly believe my own eyes when I saw their list. There was, for example, about a 12 meter pallet rack that was delivered in my carport during a holiday. Upon closer inspection, I could see there was no 12 m pallet rack in my living room.

I could easily disprove and explain all the things on the list, but it was not about them either. It was about harassment, and about taking me hostage. That way they hoped to pressure my mother to give them her shares.

They would only stop if she gave Niels full control of the company. Mom was not a fan of this, because she figured she had at least the same right to the company as Niels.

At the bailiff court meeting, I was able to explain all the items one by one. However, I had to hand in an old mobile phone that had cost DKK 1. Plus a printer that was broken.

Niels and his friend Calle tried to sit and look very serious and offended. I clearly remember the two caricatures sitting there, looking like it's the biggest case in the world.

The assistant judge was clearly annoyed by this ridiculous performance and when he went behind their backs to get something, he rolled his eyes and shook his head. I could clearly see what he was thinking, and I agreed. And I thought the same thing. How ridiculous these guys looked.

Afterwards, when Niels and Calle had left, devastated by the fact that they had not gotten more out of it. The assistant judge also asked, what kind of a performance was that?

However, it definitely did not stop there. Their madness continued. I was also reported to the tax authorities in an attempt to get me that way. I did not get my holiday pay either.

There was even more nonsense on their part, which I will not mention more of here. But I'm sure you can see how insane a hunt this had evolved into. During that period, there was almost a letter from their lawyer once a week. We spent a lot of energy and money defending ourselves. And that was also the whole plan. To drive mom and I out, and exhaust us.

It may look like I'm exaggerating here but in fact what I mention here is only a small part of both Niels' nonsense and the attacks that came during that period.

I won my tax case in the tax appeals board. I had to pay only a little tax on driving deductions because I did not have all my statements and reports. They were at the troll factory, and of course they would not hand them over to me.

THE FIRE

June 30, 1998 became a fateful day for the trolls. It was a morning like many others and yet not.

We had just put a lot of pressure on Troll Company because they owed Lajla about 500,000 Dkk. We threatened bankruptcy if she was not being paid.

Around noon that day, I received a fax from Niels with the words - ".... The day is not over yet". I remember we talked about how it was a very strange message.

At 2 PM, I was outside my office in the old troll factory, which we had an office in, to pick up something in my car. Then I see a large column of smoke rising from the other end of town. "It's up near the troll factory," I think. I hop in the car and drive up to look. I see the warehouse at the factory in flames and people from the factory running frantically out with things to save them.

I must admit my first thought was very obvious. I will not share this though. Figure out for yourself what I was thinking.

Niels told the police that it was a defective burner that had caused the fire. But their question was why did you use it when you know it is defective? How do you know it was exactly what caused the fire?

In fact, according to the information I later received from the police, the technicians already had their conclusion one or two hours after they arrived. Niels' many explanations simply didn't make sense.

Niels was also said to have later said that it must have been me who had set fire to the factory, because I was up there so quickly and was there while it was happening.

Then Niels also accused a painter from Gjøl of having done it because he had been there at the factory in the morning just before. And because he had commented that it was dangerous. The painter from Gjøl had been up at the troll factory that morning to buy some trolls. Like he often was. He saw Niels out in the warehouse with cardboard spread out on the floor, with the whole thing covered with wax. He said in surprise to Niels that it was dangerous.

Here I need to explain this process so that we have the facts in place.

To make molds for the trolls, they are first cast in natural wax. Then a copper mold is made around this wax model. These are the molds that are later used to cast the trolls in plastic.

When the wax is heated to get out of the molds again, it ignites very easily. My grandfather had had the bangs of his hair burnt off several times, and had high flames rising up from the pot of wax. So we all knew it was something we had to be VERY careful about.

At the new troll factory, we had even made a special workshop, completely without flammable materials, and with a fireproof steel door. Precisely for this work.

But for some reason, on this particular day, Niels stood OUTSIDE this fireproof space, between cardboard boxes with trolls, and with cardboard boxes scattered on the floor. There was even wax spread out all over it. Something that had never, ever happened before.

Due to Niels' claim that it could be the painter who had started the fire, the poor man was questioned several times by the police about this afterwards, and it was actually quite traumatic for him. However, the police could see he had no motive for setting a fire, so it was quickly dropped. But the painter felt very wronged, since he had been a very faithful customer for many years. He's been very, very mad at Niels ever since.

I have this information partly from the painter, and from one of the police officers I had contact with. They had asked me some questions about the company, the wax process, and many other things. They called and wanted to explain to us because we had asked for insight into what was happening. After all, Lajla was still co-owner of the company at this time.

They said they had questioned Niels a lot. Mostly because of the very different explanations he came up with. First it was a defective stove, then he did not know why, and then after that it was me and later the painter.

Although the police had a clear conclusion within the first hours, they could not prove it, because there were no witnesses. But he said they were very sure of their conclusion. All clues showed it but that was not enough. Clues can only be used in homicide cases.

I can not say who did it but I know the process and we ALL knew it was wildly flammable. So let's leave it there and I'll let you judge for yourself.

They allegedly managed to get multiple millions paid out from the insurance.

Their finances were saved and they were more than ready for new attacks, with more money for their lawyers.

CALL FROM THE POLICE

During an autumn holiday, my then wife, me and my two daughters had rented a holiday home by Slettestrand.

I clearly remember we were out for a lovely walk in the woods when I got the call. The man who calls says "That from the police. You are charged with a number of offenses. When can you come for questioning here at the police station?"

I ask what the charges are and where they come from. But the police assistant said that, "I know that very well". Which I did not know. I could figure out where it came from, but what it was I could not figure out.

I met a few days later for questioning at the police station, together with my lawyer.

The interrogation started slowly, and the officer took his time. He seemed to have a lot more patience than I had. I wanted to know what on earth they had come up with. It quickly became clear that what I was accused of were the same things I had been accused of at the bailiff court where they had NOT succeeded.

Now they tried once again with exactly the same things. Explained in exactly the same way but just topped off with an accusation of embezzlement for, as far as I remember, DKK 1.5 million.

I asked my lawyer if I was obliged to answer this nonsense, one more time. He said I was not obligated. The officer informed me that it could harm my case if I chose not to speak. I didn't care, saying that it was unbelievable that the police spent time on such absurd cases. "You are only a tool to blackmail with". I said "I will send you a written explanation and then you can spend your time on cases that matter". Then I took my jacket and went.

I spoke a lot with my grandmother about stopping this. She has 20% of the shares and could just say no and use her voting right with my mother. That way the family conflict could have been stopped. But Niels persuaded her to let it continue. "If you stop me from doing that, you'll ruin my life", Niels had told his mother. He tops it off with: "I really hope this kills Jeppe".

I made a long written explanation to the police. It was actually easy enough, because I could just copy the answer I had once sent to the bailiff's court.

I also gained insight into the documents the police had on the case, but here too there was nothing new apart from the 1.5 million. But I knew where they came from, so I was completely calm about that part.

Then a long time passed before I heard more, but one day we were sitting in our office in the middle of Gjøl. Suddenly, three police officers enter the office with a search warrant in hand.

They spend several hours seardhing EVERYTHING, and they also took all of our computers. I tell them that we can not run our company without them, but that is not their problem they say.

After they finished with the office, we drove out to where I lived and they searched my home and all my private belongings. It was all really intimidating. They do not find anything and I ask them if they can really take this seriously. But I also know they are only doing their job.

They also went through my all financial affairs without finding anything significant.

I can not help but think about what it has cost in public funding to pursue this case.

All this intense pressure had completely ruined both me and my then wife Mette. It was an excessively high stress level for many years. It eventually ruined our marriage, and we divorced in 2000 after being married for almost 12 years. My two girls Martine and Josefine were now, after having lived securely with two parents, going to be children of divorcees.

To save it all, my mother felt she had no choice but to sign off on surrendering her shares in the firm to Niels. She made this deal on the condition that the police case against me be dropped. But at the time, the case was so far along that it was not possible to stop it.

The damage was done and it would have been better if she had not signed, but she could not know that. Without this, the war would have just continued to something even more insane, and even more madness.

I was psychologically broken after this. If it was a case of something I had actually done, then it would be annoying, but then I could deal with it and accept my penalty. But in a case like this that was only blackmail based, it was really hard to deal with.

Mom felt the same way. That feeling of total injustice, and the fact that she had been thrown out of her life's work by her own brother for no reason, consumed her. Mother had been on antidepressant medication for a while, and for several years she was a shadow of her normal self.

THE POLICE TRIAL

Eventually, the police had come so far with the case (after about 2 years) that it had to go to court.

To save himself and Niels, Calle created a very "creative" plan about what Niels, and I should say in court. I do not remember exactly what it was, but only that it was explanations so wildly far out that it 100% certain would have gotten me into even bigger trouble. So, I immediately refused to agree to it. I said, "There's no way you can make me go and say that in court".

I, on the other hand, would go to court and tell the whole truth, and nothing else. I did not have a bad conscience over any of what had happened.

The police prosecutor and the judge were quite friendly and calm throughout their interrogation of me. However, they were both clearly annoyed during their interrogation of

Niels. It was just vague details that he came up with during his interrogation and he looked ridiculous. It did not fit at all with my explanations, and the confirmations of our witnesses. I think he suddenly regretted what he had set in motion.

Niels was still using the explanation that Calle had instructed him to come up with. He was probably fortunate that the judge was really tired of having to deal with this pointless case. Otherwise, he could probably easily have gotten into further trouble.

As I mentioned, the accusations were exactly the same 21 things they had tried to take me to the bailiff's court with, together with an accusation that I had committed embezzlement for about 1.5 million against the Troll Company.

The judge immediately dismissed most of the 21 charges as nonsense and did not even bother to talk about it. He said to the police prosecutor "There is nothing here - why bring it to me?". The prosecutor agreed with the judge and they dropped it immediately.

They only wanted to talk about the 1.5 million. I knew that the money existed and what was going on with it. I knew very well that the money came from the over-invoicing Niels had arranged with the factories in Hong Kong. I admitted that in court.

But I could also prove it was not money I had taken, supported by several witnesses. Fortunately, the others in the company also knew what had happened and could testify to my advantage.

So I was not convicted of any of the charges that Niels and Calle had brought. In return, I received a suspended sentence for failing to report the over-invoicing. In other words, a verdict for neglecting my duty as director of the company.

That was legally viable since a director is not only responsible to the owners - but also creditors, banks, and the government. Therefore, as director, I should have reported those irregularities. Fair enough, I could accept that.

But on the other side is it then reasonable that the person you have protected for so many years stabs you in the back, and tries to get you convicted for things he has actually done himself? I would question that quite a bit.

After all, I had only been loyal to what I had promised my grandfather in his time. To take care of Niels.

I was sentenced in court to pay around DKK 50,000 in legal costs. However, the police prosecutor told the judge that he suggested this amount should be removed, or at least reduced to half. This is because, as he said, I "had suffered enough during this long process".

It is not normal for a prosecutor to help the accused in that way, but he could see what the case was. It was not a normal case. The police had clearly been used as a tool in this blackmail. They were well aware of that.

After the case was over, I got a big hug from the police prosecutor, and he literally said "Now this witch hunt is over". He told me he would go back to the police station and file it all, and said I should now go home and start living my life. I would not hear anything more from the police about this case.

He also said that the police had actually tried to close the case several times because they could see it was a witch hunt. But each time, Niels and Calle had stubbornly insisted it should continue.

After Niels and Calle had finally got their will with the shares, they were suddenly "friendly". They even tried to lay it on thick by paying my fine / legal costs.

I was later also offered my grandmother's 20% of the shares and was also offered a seat on the company's board.

I honestly didn't know why I should be on that board. The meetings were a long monologue from Calle about all his amazing ideas and plans. The rest of us had no opportunity to provide input, since he never shut up. If we tried to say something, we were immediately interrupted. I figured it would be too risky to stay on the board. I simply did not trust what was going on and did not dare to have a board responsibility with that kind of director. So therefore, I quickly left the board again. I had had enough of their nonsense.

FORGING A NEW PATH

In the same years as the police case, I had a job as regional manager in a large Scandinavian insurance company.

This job went really well, and I had really good success with the leadership development I was in charge of. The offices I had been given responsibility for experienced a great deal of revenue growth and I had quickly become a very well-liked boss.

I had even just been offered a job at the group's headquarters in Stockholm because it was going so well. They had also offered me a top management education in London. So the future looked really bright for me.

However, due to the constant legal issues and the stress that came with it, I unfortunately had to report sick for a period of time. I could not handle a demanding managerial job, and at the same time handle the police case, and all the other legal nonsense. I had started talking incoherently in meetings, forgetting too much.

And after the end of the trial, and the verdict I received for my failure in my directorial responsibilities, the dream of this new job was extinguished very quickly. I had to stop it.

I then started my own business again, this time as an educator for coaches, and was very successful here.

At the same time, I participated in a couple of programs about stress on Danish television DR1 and DR2. I am also a co-author of a book on stress, which the Danish Health and Medicines Authority publishes. I also travel around the country during these years and give lectures in collaboration with the Psychiatric Foundation.

At the same time, I also wrote my own book about stress and how to overcome it.

As I had become more geographically independent with my online business, I moved to Mallorca in 2007. After all that has happened, I just needed the change of pace. I needed a total change of air after those years of really traumatic experiences.

THE MOVIE

It's always been my grandfather's big dream to get the trolls in a movie. One of his great role models was the Norwegian animated film Bjergkøbing Grand Prix made by Ivo Caprino.

For many years he worked diligently to make a movable troll for this. He made many prototypes, but unfortunately without success. After watching a new Disney animated film, he totally abandons this dream. "I cannot keep up with that", he says.

Fortunately, this later became possible and in 2010 the possibilities for a film began to emerge again.

There were several film companies interested, but the most exciting was Dreamworks which had made the film Shrek among others.

Again we had to work together, thankfully not very closely. Lajla and Niels had inherited the artist rights (also called Intellectual property) to the Trolls from their father, and therefore Niels and Calle - probably to their great regret - again had to collaborate with us again.

Without our permission, a film contract could not be made, so our interference was inevitable.

During this contract negotiations I always only received the most necessary information and was only used when absolutely necessary.

Lajla had handed over the rights to me so that I could manage them a few years earlier. She would rather avoid having to collaborate with either Calle or Niels again. So, it was I who had to make agreements with them. Mom would rather have nothing at all to do with those two.

It is very rare for my mother to say something bad about other people, but when she talks about Calle, one can really hear how much pain that man has caused her. So she would rather hand it over to me to deal with.

It was a long tough job and required a lot of patience. But eventually the deal was finally signed in 2012, and Dreamworks paid a record amount for the rights.

MY TROLL LIFE

In 2016, the film premiered the movie TROLLS was a reality. I really love the movie and I am sure my grandfather is somewhere (with all his friends) and smiling. Dreamworks did such a good job with the trolls. They don't look totally like the classic trolls – but they certainly have the mindset and the vibe that Thomas would have given them.

Unfortunately, I was unable to attend this first premiere due to a surgery. Two years later Trolls 2 came out.

CONCLUSION...

Niels' good friend, Calle Østergaard, is in my eyes a person who saw an opportunity to come in and make money at the expense of the family. He saw he could use Niels' anger to create a place for himself. He loves legal disputes and has clearly been like a fish in water with this whole process.

Before my mother was thrown out of the factory, he met a lot at Niels' home, as previously mentioned, and big plans were drawn up. Without that help, Niels would never have been able to throw Lajla out of the factory, and start this war with us.

Yes, he made a great effort in connection with the Trolls movie. I'll give him credit for that. But the way he works is another story.

In my world, there is absolutely nothing that justifies someone destroying someone else for personal gain.

To say "I hope this kills Jeppe" as Niels said to his mom, is far beyond normal behavior. How is it possible to hate so much? And to Niels fortune he had found a person with absolutely no limits as a partner.

Is it ok to ruin Lajla's life and her life's work just to get something for yourself?

As for me, it was fine to stop a manager. It happens all the time that you stop in jobs if something doesn't work. But I can't comprehend how that's not enough. Why its necessary that you would go after a person with the hopes of destroying them completely.

Thomas created the trolls as something really positive, and it was his clear wish that it should be continued by his entire family. He said this several times before he died. He rejoiced that he had created something that could benefit the whole family.

In recent years, Lajla and I have been written almost out of the story of the trolls. Lajla a little bit, and I more or less completely. When there is mention of the Trolls' story we are omitted or mentioned only with offhand remarks.

This is despite the fact that the trolls would not in any way have become what they are now, without our work over many years.

Niels on the other hand has made NO effort to make them what they are today. When they started, he was a little boy. And all he did was hinder the company's progress. Niels and Calle simply do not accept when this important part of the story is mentioned by anyone. Niels gets fiery furious when he only hears my name mentioned.

For the premiere of the Trolls films, we were allowed to participate probably because the distributor wanted it. However, I was ill and could not participate but Lajla, Martine and Josefine attended the premiere.

But otherwise we have been kept totally out of the loop about this. Niels, Calle, and his family had been invited to the other events that had been held.

We have been non-existent throughout this process. My two daughters Martine and Josefine have often asked if they could not come to some of the many events that have been held in connection with the Trolls films. But every time we asked, we received no answer.

Niels was many times helped by his mother Betty and her 20% ownership share, to be able to continue to get us pushed out of the company. As mentioned earlier, she could easily have stopped the split, but every single time, Niels convinced her.

Despite her help, Niels did not visit her once in the last many years of her life. He had gotten what he wanted and saw no reason to visit her anymore. Despite being close by, he did not go up to visit her once. Betty said many times she could not understand that he didn't visit. The last few years she suffered from dementia and could not tell the difference between us, and several times thought I was Niels when I visited her. That made her a little bit happier.

The only person who really helped Betty her final years was Lajla, who faithfully was there every single day. When she asked if Niels would help, he replied that he did not care. When Betty died, however, Niels showed up very quickly at her apartment to take the things he wanted that Thomas had owned. But after that he also refused to help clean up her apartment.

AM I BITTER? NO.

This whole last part of the story might paint me as a bitter person but that's not how it is.

The story is written as it happened, and I do not want to embellish it more than I have done.

I know I sound angry in the last chapters but it's nothing compared to what we've had to deal with all these years. Its not possible to depict the intensity and madness in this conflict.

I think there must be justice and I want to make sure that the TRUE story is told. It may seem like I'm exaggerating but on the contrary.

If we look at what Niels has actually done, which I do NOT write about, then it could fill an entire book for itself. This is just a selection of the exciting highlights. The other things I COULD write would completely ruin Niels and Calle's lives - and I do not want that.

THANKS TO THOMAS DAM

This book is written out of my deep gratitude for what I have been able to help create. I'm super proud to have experienced all of this, along with the amazing person that my grandfather Thomas was.

I am proud of the strength and perseverance my mother Lajla has always shown. Her strength as a very young person to have the foresight to be able to see that the Trolls could become something very big. I'm proud she always believed in me and the eternal trust enabled me to accomplish all the things we did together, to get the Trolls become the success that they did.

I'm really proud when I see what a positive impact Grandpa's Trolls have on a lot of people around the world.

With this book, I hoped both the success and also the negative aspects of this story should come to light.

There is the modest start of Thomas' life. From poverty to his success. His struggle to survive and the challenges with the Trolls. Not just once, but several times.

Success is usually measured in money, but his success with the trolls is much more. The real success story is the joy his Trolls give people. It is something that money cannot buy.

In almost every success story, there is always a flip side to the coin. There was certainly the case with the Trolls.

Lajla has never come completely gotten over all that has happened. She is a positive person but still has a hard time understanding why there can be so much hate. I still suffer a lot from serious mental problems from the many years of drama and have periods I can not work. But I've got a good life again in spite of that. I have a great relationship and finally feel happy again. I have started several different companies.

That's why I'm happy to finally be able to tell the whole story. And take that weight off my shoulders.

We must always keep in mind that in order to be light, there must also be darkness. The Trolls bring lots of light into human lives. The dark side of the Trolls has been a couple of incredibly small-minded people whose greed was not able to be tamed.

But as always, the light wins. The good triumphs again, and the two will not be able to influence the magic of the Trolls. The Trolls live on for a long time even after these two people are long gone.

The trolls adventure lives on thanks to all the fantastic Troll fans.

END

Made in the USA
Monee, IL
05 June 2023